BEAUTIFUL BLUE
& YOU

By

Michael Richardson and

Dr. Melinda Lincoln Richardson

Dedication

We wish to thank our family and friends for their love and support during this project of unique creativity. Thank you, Michael, for your keen eye and observation of Beautiful Blue and for capturing the wonder of nature at its best.

Also, thank you, Mindy, for utilizing your special talents and word choice to capture the reflection of life through nature with each narration. Life is so fulfilling when enhanced by natural beauty.

Preface

In this gallery of live photos captured by Michael, you will feel a sense of excitement and contentment within the aura of the Blue Heron. The strength, stability, and the need to survive provides a roadmap for the reader to enjoy the unique experience of each virtual photo. Just "being" alive is a tell-tale sign of fulfillment and following your lifetime journey.

Enjoy the beautiful moments and apply strength and determination to your life on your road to fulfillment. After all, nature reflects the basics in life we all need to live and thrive. May we empower you with beauty and thought as you live each day through the eyes of endless wonder.

Apply the lessons in life, through the narrations, to better your choices and find contentment along the way.

Wishing you joy, insight, and peace as you journey through life.

Cheers,

Michael and Melinda

2

Life is a continuous stream of challenges. See clearly, for the waters are buoyant with energy, endless possibilities, and unexpected outcomes. Choose wisely, my friend.

Determined to achieve my goal. Be swift, direct, and

expedient. Life is short.

A firm stance on life provides the strength to make

greater choices. Follow the path that delivers the best

results.

Unafraid. Blue on blue provides the essence of my being.

Accept reality and make it greater.

Past lessons lead to the reality of the moment. Wisdom

filters weaknesses and provides a sense of well-being.

Solace.

Reflections in life are empowering. Senses are sharp and direct a journey forward. Stay the course.

Small steps yield powerful results. Never turn away from

an unknown future. Set your sights high.

Embrace life fully. Understand your limits, but recognize

the undeniable power to be yourself. You are beautiful.

Life is a combination of wishes and dreams. Your

perspective will take you to the destiny ahead. Plan your

course and enjoy the journey.

Ready, set, go. Never finish last, but keep pace with the world. Appreciate your strengths, for they will lead you through life's journeys and take you to the finish line.

Spread your wings. Life is a flight of trials and

tribulations. Never knowing the future, but building the

skills and talents to move you forward with

determination and success.

Share your aura. Each of us has much to share with

others. Hold loved ones under your wings and

provide love, strength, and a continuous eagerness to

fulfill their journey in life.

Blue is Blue. Perched on a rock illustrates a dynamic

spirit with dimension and perseverance. A leader is born.

Drying off. Never be the least of your abilities. Push your

talents to the best part of your existence. Enjoy the

rewards for a lifetime.

Aware and ready. Life presents an array of challenges and surprises. Be prepared to face the unexpected with grace and dignity.

Eyes on the world. Look for the importance of life. Review

your relevance and make the best move. Enhance the

living.

Blue meets world. Ready to activate life's call and join the

wonders of nature. Simply, be yourself. You are stunning.

Beautiful in Blue. Make your mark on the world with great satisfaction. The gift you make to others will satisfy and be greatly appreciated.

Race you. Never knowing when to stop, keep striving for

your best. Whether today or tomorrow, greatness is

nearby.

Clear as a bell. When the road ahead presents a new direction, rely on your keen sense of truth and understanding. Taking the right stand provides new opportunities and options in life.

Poised to succeed. Move forward with anticipation,

excitement, and hope for the future. Life is a strange

combination of emotions and reactions which make

you complete.

Be one with yourself and understand nature. Beauty is

all around us. Home is where your heart lies.

The light is right. Choices will appear in the break of the day. Choose wisely and reap the benefits of your choices.

Over the bridge and through the woods. Your next

journey awaits. Are you impatient to leave your mark on

the world?

Splendor in the grass. The essence of our being is
unique. Share the best of yourself with others. Life is full
of wonder and beauty.

Standing tall. Be brave, be keen, and be alert to any danger. Composure will measure your abilities to deal with life. Make the best choices possible. Always.

Off to lunch. Never hesitate to nourish yourself with the

pleasures of life. Moments move quickly. Later.

Spotted again. Framed and ready for action. Images last

forever, followed by smart decisions. Know your

strengths and recognize possibilities.

About to launch. Flight is a necessary process for one's

destiny. Enjoy the journey.

Finding a strong voice. Speak your thoughts and support

your actions. Your ambitions will make your dreams a

reality. Always.

Blue Heron in flight. Flying high and determined to lead

your best life. No bounds to the journey ahead. Take aim

and reap the treasures that await.

Delicate but strong. Looking over all of us with thought

and wisdom brings peace and contentment. The world

will celebrate with joy.

The spray is refreshing. Feel the rejuvenation of life with

every thought, movement, and direction. Enjoy the

journey.

High on life. Balance all concerns with the reality of the

moment. Enjoy the freedom of thought and freedom of

choice. You are mighty.

Standing alone, but unafraid. Courage provides a

remarkable sense of confidence. Move forward with

resilience and tenacity to find your way. Perfect.

Time to think. When in doubt, know that honest contemplation is a gift of nature. Life depends on sound choices and accurate decisions.

Beautiful and whole. Be your best with the world. Always stay the course and reap the benefits of achievement.

Separate, but never alone. Building your future

strengthens your inner being. Sharing strength with

others is a true gift for all.

Beautiful Blue. This royal color combination will help to

see life from many perspectives. Strength is a gift earned.

Appreciate the beauty of nature. Live.

Trendsetter. Leaders are meant to be followed. They lead others to be the best at hand. Never retreat. Stay strong.

Small steps, big gains. Be steady and cautious on your path. Your destination will be reached with greater purpose and clarity than thought possible.

On the brink of life. On the brink of love. On the brink of

peaceful solitude. Nothing better. Enjoy the precious

moments.

Majestic, indeed. The company you keep inspires the

best. Always be ready for the unexpected.

Self-reflection. Often, deep thought will provide greater

insight into your psyche. Knowing yourself is a mystical

gift to be treasured, never neglected.

91

Time to think. When in doubt, know that honest

contemplation is a gift of nature.

Life depends on sound choices and accurate decisions.

Enjoy the walk to your destiny.

Never turn away from an opportunity to learn and grow.

Appreciate the moments to share nature and to

understand life.

Steady and secure in life. Confidence will carry

us through the high and the low moments which build

our destiny. Life is sweet and swift.

Looking through an opening of new beginnings. The

path ahead embodies many choices and decisions

affecting approaching journeys. Life awaits.

Reflections urge us forward. Not knowing what is ahead,

rely on courage to lead to best practices. The future is

beautiful.

Rocky starts, smooth path. Never wander too far

off nature's trail in life. The path may never open to us

again. It may lead to the most unexpected experiences of

our journey.

The ascent begins. Every step is cautiously planned. Your roadmap to the future is a single step followed by the next. Be secure in your presence, and all will fall into place.

Off to dine. An acquired taste for the unique and a zest for life has evolved. Enjoy the different textures and the delicacy of something new. Form your future.

Ready for lunch surrounded by nature's beauty.

Share with others who embrace the beauty and the clear

aura of the moment.

Perfect spot for lunch. Surrounded by nature, appreciate

the warmth of the day. Sunshine fills our being with joy

and warmth. Always.

Tiny turtle appetizers support the cycle of life. Eat well and prosper. The cycle of life is constant and feeds the mind, body, and soul.

Life is a continuous journey with choices. Choose wisely and live life to the fullest. Unexpected wonders suddenly occur.

Turtle soup is on the menu tonight. Try new tastes and

take bold directions to achieve your goals. All is well.

Stepping out in style. Looking fit, sharp, and confident at every turn. Be yourself empowered with lasting strength for a lifetime.

Busy eating. Feed the natural energy of nature and

accumulate all that you can be. One day at a time

becomes a measure of living a worthy life well.

Good fishing hole. Know your surroundings and rely on

past experiences to support the new. Your reality is the

truth.

A little to the left, please. Know your photogenic side. Put

your best foot forward to achieve your goals and

aspirations. Looking good.

Can't resist. Tiny turtles are high in protein. Keeping up one's strength is important to overall health, function, and longevity. Bon Appetite!

Be yourself. Whether young or old, blue or green, see

beauty in all living souls. Cherish the moment.

Nature at its best. Grace, charm, and dignity are front

and center. Comport yourself with confidence and pride.

Always.

Looking good from all angles. Appreciate the beauty

created by your being. Life is better by recognizing many

perspectives. Live each moment fully.

Blue beauty. Stepping out in life with vitality, resilience,

and energy. Feel proud of your legacy. Always.

Tea for two. The best moment in life is sharing with others. Interaction is a key ingredient to learning from others and giving back unconditionally.

Not by a long shot. Accept the challenge without fear or

intimidation. Know that the best is yet to come. Life is

calling...

I'm winning. Sometimes, I move ahead in the stream of life. Other times, I admire those leading the path for me to follow. Stay close.

Coming out of the shadows. Never be afraid of who you are. Stand tall and address life's challenges. New beginnings lead to golden opportunities not to be missed.

Remarkable Blue. Represent the quality of life. Always looking for more to complement the surrounding aura. The search for greater understanding becomes us in so many wonderful ways.

Life is better with friends. Whether small or large, we

are whole interacting with others. Learning, laughing,

and just being becomes us.

Jewel of the Nile. Glorious moment. Cherish the air, the

current, and the journeys to follow.

Crystal clear. A rainbow of color spins the beauty of

nature at its best. Diversity brings the strength of

character to each of us in our own way.

Never let a day go by unnoticed. The beauty of a moment

needs to be savored. Taste the glory of life.

Accept us for who we are. Embrace the beauty of life

standing before our eyes. We are on the same team.

Learn from one another. Always.

Reflective insight. Deep thought and intrigue surround

us. New ideas and thoughts flow from our being

constantly. Creativity is boundless . . .

Ripples touch us all. Never standing solely alone, feel the need to be with others. A single thought touches many lives daily and joyfully.

Double the fun. Our image is reflected in the eyes of others. Role models are the pillars of strength to build the best in life for others.

The skylight shines on the water and reveals the path ahead. See the light as you journey forward to the next season with contentment and peace. Farewell, my friend.

Treading carefully. Life is a tripod of color, intrigue, and mystery. Choose wisely and enjoy the outcome. Rainbows are beautiful creations to share.

Upright and ready. Instinctual behavior comes from within. Open your mind and give with your heart. Your rewards are endless.

The falls ignite a fullness deep inside. To live. To

survive. Welcome home!

An eye on the world! Our journey is closing on a perfect evening. Count your blessings and just be you, for that is enough.

About the Authors

Michael Richardson PE

Michael is a retired Professional Engineer with a career spanning service as an Army officer, an industrial engineering manager, a designer and builder of US Embassies, and an operational test director for the Department of Homeland Security. Taking up photography in retirement, he captures the natural beauty of his home's environment as well as many of the images of life in Williamsburg, Virginia. A small pond near his home enticed a Blue Heron and many other waterfowl to model for his benefit and for your enjoyment. The joy of sharing these images provides the motivation to record new experiences every day.

Dr. Melinda Lincoln-Richardson

Melinda is an educator, teacher, and professor with advanced degrees in English, Speech, Drama, Professional Teaching Studies, Mediation, and a Doctoral of Arts Degree in Communication. Her first published book, *Conflict Resolution Communication: Patterns Promoting Peaceful Schools*, published by Rowman & Littlefield, presents a solid option for safe and peaceful schools. Additionally, she served as a Program Manager for the Department of Education and an Ombudsman and a Senior Policy Advisor for the Department of Homeland Security.

Challenging her creative abilities, Melinda channeled her stream of consciousness and applied narrations to enhance the essence of each photo captured in BEAUTIFUL BLUE & YOU. She believes a joint collaboration with her husband is a gift to be shared with others.

CPSIA information can be obtained
at www.ICGtesting.com
Printed in the USA
BVHW012156291222
655298BV00028B/499